Table of contents
p.no.

Introduction: Welcome to the Stock Market

- **What is the stock market?**

Hey there, 10-year-old investor-to-be! The stock market is like a big store where people buy and sell tiny pieces of ownership in companies. Imagine you have a favorite candy shop, and you really love their delicious candies. Now, let's say that a candy shop decides to become a big company with lots of candy stores all around the country.

When they become a big company, they split themselves into tiny pieces, and each piece is called a "stock." These stocks are like little shares of the company. So, when you buy a stock, it means you own a tiny piece of that candy company.

Now, the stock market is where people come together to trade these tiny pieces (stocks) with each other. Some people want to buy the stocks because they believe the company will do well and grow, just like you think the candy shop will get more popular. And some people want to sell their stocks because they might need the money or feel the company won't do well anymore.

The prices of these stocks can go up and down, just like how the price of your favorite candy might change if it becomes really popular or if people stop liking it. People try to make smart decisions about when to buy and sell stocks so they can hopefully make some money.

So, in a nutshell, the stock market is like a big trading place where people buy and sell tiny pieces of companies they believe will do well. It's a bit like trading candies, but instead, we trade tiny pieces of companies to make money and grow our savings! Cool, right? ☐

- **Why is investing important?**

Hey there, little investor! Investing is like planting seeds in a garden, but instead of growing plants, you grow your money. Here's why it's essential:

1. Making Money Grow: When you invest your money, it has the potential to grow over time. Just like a tiny seed becomes a big tree, your money can become more significant if you invest it wisely.

2. Beating Inflation: Inflation is like a sneaky bug that makes things cost more over time. When you keep your money in a piggy bank, it may not grow as fast as the prices of things around you. But when you invest, you have a better chance of keeping up with inflation.

3. Reaching Goals: Maybe you want to buy a cool toy, go on a fun trip, or save for college in the future. Investing can help you reach those goals by making your money work harder for you.

4. Learning About the World: When you invest, you become a part-owner of companies. It's like being a superhero of businesses! You get to learn how companies work, what they sell, and how they make money.

5. Patience and Planning: Investing teaches you to be patient and plan for the future. Just like a tree takes time to grow, your investments may take time to grow too.

6. Financial Freedom: When you grow your money through investing, you may not need to depend on others as much. You'll have more control over your finances and more options for what you want to do in life.

Chapter 1: The Basics of Investing

- **What is an investment?**

Hey there, curious mind! An investment is like planting a magical money seed. When you have some extra money, instead of spending it all on toys or candies, you can put it into something special called an "investment."

Now, imagine you put that money seed into a special pot called a "bank account" or a "piggy bank." When you keep it there, something amazing happens! That little money seed starts to grow slowly over time, just like a plant growing taller and taller.

But here's the best part: The more time you give it, the more it grows! You see, investments are like patient friends that grow with time, and they can help you have even more money later on.

You might wonder, "What kind of magical pot is this?" Well, there are different types of magical pots for investments. Some are like little pieces of ownership in big companies, just like owning a tiny bit of your favorite store. Others are like lending your money to someone, and they pay you back with a little extra as a thank-you gift.

The most important thing to remember is that investments are a way to make your money grow over time, so you can have more choices and do exciting things in the future. And like any great adventure, it's good to have grown-ups, like your parents or guardians, to help you with your investment journey.

- Different types of investments (stocks, bonds, etc.)

Sure thing, little investor! Let's explore the different types of investments using some fun and easy-to-understand examples:

1. Stocks: Stocks are like magical ownership potions! When you buy a stock, you become a part-owner of a company you like. It's a bit like having a small piece of your favorite toy store or candy shop. As the company grows and becomes more popular, your ownership potion (stock) may become more valuable, just like how your favorite toys become more precious to you.

2. Bonds: Bonds are like friendly loans to others. When you buy a bond, you are lending your money to a company or even the government! They promise to pay you back your money with a little extra as a thank-you for lending it to them. It's like being a good friend who helps others and gets a little reward in return.

3. Mutual Funds: Mutual funds are like teamwork with your friends. Imagine you and your friends all put your money together to buy lots of different toys. Each friend owns a little part of all the toys. That's how mutual funds work! They collect money from many people and invest it in different stocks and bonds to help you become a part-owner of many companies.

4. Real Estate: Real estate is like owning a magical land. You know how you build a castle in your sandbox or playhouse? Well, when you buy real estate, you own a piece of land or a building. People pay you rent to use that land or building, just like your friends paying you for playing in your castle. It's a smart way to make money from your magical land!

5. Savings Account: A savings account is like a treasure box for your money. When you save your money in a bank, they keep it safe for you and even give you a little prize called "interest" on top of your money! It's like earning extra candies just for keeping your money safe in their treasure box.

Remember, each type of investment has its own magic, and you can choose the ones that feel right for you and your adventure.

- **The concept of risk and return.**

Sure thing, little investor! Let's imagine you're going on an exciting adventure in a magical forest.

1. Risk: Risk is like the unexpected twists and turns you might encounter in the forest adventure. Some paths may be smooth and easy, while others could have obstacles or surprises. Similarly, in

investments, risk means there's a chance that your money might not grow as much as you hope. Some investments may go up a lot, like a roller coaster ride, but others might not go up much at all, like a slow train.

2. Return: Return is like the rewards and treasures you find on your forest adventure. When you take a risk and make a wise investment, your money can grow bigger, just like finding a pot of gold or precious gems in the forest. The return is how much extra money you get from your investment when it becomes more valuable.

Now, here's the exciting part! In the magical forest of investments, the bigger the risk you take, the bigger the rewards you might find. It's like climbing a tall tree to see a beautiful view from the top!

But, remember that some paths in the forest might be too risky, like crossing a shaky bridge, and you might lose some money. So, it's essential to be smart and choose your adventures wisely.

A good idea is to have a mix of different adventures, like trying a few exciting paths and some safer ones. This way, you can have fun exploring, but you won't lose all your candies if something unexpected happens.

Just like in the forest adventure, it's a great idea to have your parents or guardians as your adventure guides in the world of investments. They can help you understand the risks and rewards, so you can have a magical and successful investment journey!

Chapter 2: All About Stocks

- What are stocks?

Stocks are like magical ownership potions for companies. Let me explain:

Imagine you have a favorite candy shop that sells the yummiest candies in the whole town. Now, this candy shop decides to become a big company with lots of candy shops all over the country.

When they become a big company, they split themselves into tiny pieces, and each piece is called a "stock." These stocks are like little potions of ownership in the candy company. So, when you buy a stock, it means you own a tiny piece of that candy company.

Now, here's where the magic happens! When the candy company does well, and more people want to buy their candies, the value of your tiny ownership potion (stock) goes up. It's like having a special potion that becomes more powerful and valuable as the candy company grows and becomes more popular.

But, just like in any adventure, there might be some ups and downs. Sometimes, the candy company might face challenges or competition, and the value of your potion might go down a bit. But don't worry! Just like a brave adventurer, you can decide to keep your potion and wait for it to grow again.

So, owning stocks is like being a part-owner of your favorite candy shop and cheering for its success. It's a fun way to grow your money and become a little boss of a real company!

- Famous companies and their stocks.

I can provide you with some examples of famous large-cap companies in India and their past performance till the time i started writing this book.

1. Reliance Industries Limited (RIL):
- Industry: Diversified (including oil, gas, retail, and telecommunications)
- Stock Symbol: RELIANCE
- Past Performance: RIL has been one of India's largest and most valuable companies. Its stock has shown significant growth over the years, driven by the company's expansion into various sectors and strong financial performance.

2. Tata Consultancy Services Limited (TCS):
- Industry: IT Services
- Stock Symbol: TCS
- Past Performance: TCS is a leading IT services company and a flagship of the Tata group. Its stock has experienced steady growth, fueled by the demand for technology services globally and its consistent financial performance.

3. Hindustan Unilever Limited (HUL):
- Industry: Consumer Goods
- Stock Symbol: HINDUNILVR
- Past Performance: HUL is a renowned consumer goods company with well-known brands. Its stock has exhibited stable growth over time due to the company's strong market presence and popular product offerings.

4. HDFC Bank Limited:
- Industry: Banking and Financial Services
- Stock Symbol: HDFCBANK

- Past Performance: HDFC Bank is one of India's leading private sector banks. Its stock has historically shown impressive growth, attributed to its robust financial performance and a strong presence in the banking industry.

5. Infosys Limited:
- Industry: IT Services
- Stock Symbol: INFY
- Past Performance: Infosys is a prominent IT services company in India. Its stock has witnessed fluctuations, influenced by changes in the IT sector and global economic conditions. However, it has generally shown positive performance over the years.

Please note that stock performance is subject to market fluctuations, economic conditions, and company-specific factors. Past performance does not guarantee future results, and it is crucial to conduct thorough research and seek advice from financial experts before making any investment decisions. For the latest and most accurate information, it is best to consult financial sources and official stock market data.

- **Understanding stock prices and ticker symbols.**

Understanding stock prices and ticker symbols is like learning a secret code to know how much a company's ownership potion (stock) is worth and what its name is. Let me break it down for you:

1. Stock Prices: Imagine you have a favorite candy company, and you want to know how much one tiny ownership potion (stock) of that company is worth. That's where stock prices come in! The stock price tells you the magic number you need to pay to buy one tiny potion of ownership.

- If the stock price is high, it means the tiny ownership potion is quite expensive, like buying a fancy toy.
- If the stock price is low, it means the tiny ownership potion is more affordable, like buying a simple treat.

2. Ticker Symbols: Now, here comes the secret code part! Every company has a unique nickname called a "ticker symbol." It's like a special name tag for the company's ownership potions (stocks).

- For example, if the candy company's name is "Yummy Candies Limited," its ticker symbol might be "YCL." It's like a secret code that helps you quickly identify the company.

So, when you see "YCL" with a stock price next to it, you'll know that it's the code for your favorite candy company's ownership potions and how much each tiny potion costs.

Remember, these secret codes and prices change every day, just like the prices of your favorite candies at the store.

Chapter 3: How to Buy Stocks

- **Choosing a brokerage account.**

Choosing a brokerage account is an important decision as it will be your gateway to buying and selling stocks and other financial instruments. Here are some steps to help you choose a brokerage account that suits your needs:

1. Research Different Brokers: Start by researching different brokerage firms in India. Look for well-established and reputable brokers that have a good track record. Check online reviews and ask for recommendations from friends or family who have experience with investing.

2. Compare Fees and Charges: Different brokerage firms may have varying fees and charges for their services. Some common charges include brokerage fees (commission on trades), account maintenance fees, and transaction charges. Compare these fees to find a broker that offers competitive rates.

3. Trading Platform and Tools: Check out the broker's trading platform and tools. A user-friendly and intuitive platform will make it easier for you to buy and sell stocks. Look for features like real-time market data, research reports, and technical analysis tools.

4. Account Types: Consider the types of accounts the broker offers. Most brokers provide individual accounts, joint accounts, and sometimes even special accounts for minors. Choose one that best fits your requirements.

5. Customer Service: Good customer service is crucial, especially for beginners. Look for a broker that provides prompt and reliable customer support through phone, email, or live chat.

6. Research and Educational Resources: As a novice investor, educational resources and research materials are essential. Some brokers offer educational materials, webinars, and tutorials to help you understand investing better.

7. Mobile App: Check if the broker has a mobile app that allows you to trade on the go. A mobile app can be convenient for monitoring your investments and making quick decisions.

8. Security: Ensure that the brokerage firm has robust security measures in place to protect your account and personal information.

9. Account Opening Process: Review the account opening process. Some brokers may have a straightforward online application process, while others may require physical documents. Choose one that is convenient for you.

10. Regulatory Compliance: Ensure that the broker is registered with the Securities and Exchange Board of India (SEBI), the regulatory authority for the securities market in India.

Remember, it's essential to take your time and choose a brokerage account that aligns with your investment goals, risk tolerance, and level of experience. If you're unsure, seek guidance from a financial advisor or someone experienced in investing.

- **Placing your first stock order.**

Placing your first stock order in the stock market is like buying a tiny ownership potion (stock) of a company you believe in. It may seem a bit daunting at first, but don't worry—I'll guide you through the steps:

Step 1: Choose a Brokerage Account
To begin, you need a brokerage account. Think of it as a magical store where you can buy and sell stocks. Choose a brokerage firm that you feel comfortable with and that offers the features you need.

Step 2: Research the Company
Before you buy a stock, learn about the company you want to invest in. Check its financial health, products or services, and how well it is doing in the market. Just like knowing your favorite toy or candy inside out, it's essential to understand the company you want to invest in.

Step 3: Decide on the Number of Shares
Next, decide how many tiny ownership potions (shares) you want to buy. The more shares you buy, the bigger your ownership in the company. But remember, only buy as many as you can afford and be comfortable holding for the long term.

Step 4: Choose the Order Type
When you're ready to make the purchase, you have two common order types:

- Market Order: This is like saying, "I want to buy the stock right now at whatever price it is currently trading." It's quick and easy, but the stock's price may fluctuate slightly between the time you place the order and when it gets executed.

- Limit Order: This is like setting a maximum price you're willing to pay for the stock. You'll say, "I want to buy the stock, but only if the price is below a specific amount." It may take a bit longer to execute, but you have more control over the price you pay.

Step 5: Place the Order
Now it's time to place your order with your brokerage firm. You can do this online or by calling your broker. Provide them with the company's name or its special code (ticker symbol), the number of shares you want, and the type of order you choose.

Step 6: Monitor Your Investment
Congratulations! You're now a proud owner of tiny ownership potions in a real company. Remember, the stock's price may go up and down, just like a roller coaster. Keep an eye on your investment, but don't let short-term fluctuations worry you. Investing is usually for the long term, like growing a beautiful garden.

- **Understanding market orders and limit orders.**

Understanding market orders and limit orders is like choosing different ways to buy your favorite toys from a store. Let's explore each type:

1. Market Order: Imagine you walk into a toy store, and you see a toy you really want. You go straight to the cashier and say, "I want to buy this toy right now at whatever price it is."

In the stock market, a market order works the same way. When you place a market order, you're telling your broker, "I want to buy this stock right now at the current market price." The broker will try to find the best available price for you and execute the order as quickly as possible.

Pros:
- Quick Execution: Market orders are usually executed immediately, so you get the stock right away.
- Certainty: You are guaranteed to get the stock, even if the price changes slightly by the time the order is executed.

Cons:

- Price Fluctuations: Since you accept the current market price, the final price you pay might be slightly different from the price you saw when you placed the order.

2. Limit Order: Now, let's say you visit the toy store, but you're not in a hurry to buy the toy. Instead, you decide on the highest price you're willing to pay for it. You tell the cashier, "I want to buy this toy, but only if it costs less than $20."

A limit order in the stock market is similar. You specify the highest price you're willing to pay for a stock. When you place a limit order, you're telling your broker, "I want to buy this stock, but only if it's available at or below a certain price."

Pros:
- Price Control: With a limit order, you have more control over the price you pay for the stock.
- Patience: You can wait for the stock's price to come down to your desired level before buying.

Cons:
- Execution Not Guaranteed: Unlike market orders, limit orders may not get executed immediately if the stock's price doesn't reach your specified limit.

Remember, both market orders and limit orders have their uses. Market orders are great when you want to buy the stock right away, while limit orders are useful when you're patient and want to control the price you pay.

As you grow as an investor, you'll learn when to use each order type to make the most of your investments.

Chapter 4: The Power of Long-Term Investing

- **What is long-term investing?**

Long-term investing is like planting a money tree that grows and bears fruits over a long period of time. Instead of expecting quick results like a magical potion, long-term investing is about having patience and letting your money grow steadily like a strong tree.

Here's how it works:

1. Planting the Seed: When you invest your money in a long-term investment, you're buying tiny ownership potions (stocks) of companies or other assets you believe will grow in value over many years.

2. Nurturing the Investment: Just like you water and take care of a young plant, you'll keep your investments safe and sometimes add more money to help them grow stronger.

3. Allowing Time to Work Magic: The magic of long-term investing happens over time. As the companies you invest in grow and become more successful, the value of your tiny ownership potions (stocks) may increase.

4. Reaping the Fruits: When the time is right, you can enjoy the fruits of your long-term investment. You might sell some of your tiny ownership potions at a higher price than you bought them, just like harvesting ripe fruits from your money tree.

The key to long-term investing is to be patient and not get worried about short-term ups and downs, just like a wise wizard who knows that the magic of the money tree takes time to show its full power.

Long-term investing is like a slow and steady adventure that can help you achieve your financial goals, like saving for college, buying a dream house, or having a magical retirement. So, plant your money tree early, nurture it with regular investments, and watch it grow into something truly magical over the years!

- **The magic of compounding.**

The magic of compounding is like a spell that makes your money grow faster and faster over time. It's one of the most powerful tools in the world of investing. Let me show you how it works with a magical example:

Imagine you have a magical money potion that doubles in size every year. At first, you have one coin, but after one year, it becomes two coins. After the second year, those two coins become four, and after the third year, those four coins become eight. The potion keeps doubling and growing with each passing year!

Now, here's where the magic gets exciting. The more time you give the potion to work, the faster it grows. So, after ten years, that one tiny coin would have transformed into a whopping 1,024 coins! And after twenty years, it would become an enormous 1,048,576 coins!

This is the magic of compounding at play in the world of investing. When you invest your money, it has the potential to earn you extra money called "returns." Over time, those returns also start to earn their own returns, and this cycle continues, making your money grow like a snowball rolling down a hill, getting bigger and bigger with each roll.

The longer you keep your money invested, the more powerful the compounding magic becomes. That's why starting early in your investment journey is essential. Even tiny amounts invested consistently can grow into a substantial fortune over time, thanks to the magic of compounding.

Just remember, like any good spell, it's essential to be patient and let the magic of compounding work its wonders over the long term.

So, start your investment adventure early, keep adding to it regularly, and watch your money grow magically!

- Famous investors and their success stories.

Two famous investors in India and their success stories are:

1. Rakesh Jhunjhunwala:
Rakesh Jhunjhunwala is often referred to as the "Big Bull" of the Indian stock market. He is a well-known and successful investor with a remarkable track record. His investment journey began in the late 1980s, and he made his first significant success by investing in Tata Tea (now Tata Consumer Products).

One of his most famous success stories was his investment in Titan Company Limited, India's leading jewelry and watch retailer. He bought a significant stake in Titan when it was relatively unknown, and the stock's value soared over the years as the company expanded its market presence and product range.

Rakesh Jhunjhunwala's investment philosophy revolves around long-term value investing, identifying strong businesses with growth potential, and having the conviction to hold onto his investments even during market fluctuations.

2. Radhakishan Damani:
Radhakishan Damani, often called the "Retail King of India," is another highly successful investor and entrepreneur. He founded DMart, a chain of hypermarkets known for its low-cost, high-quality products. Under his leadership, DMart became one of the most successful retail chains in India.

Apart from his retail ventures, Damani is renowned for his astute investing in the stock market. He is known for his ability to identify undervalued companies with growth prospects. His investments in companies like VST Industries and Sundaram Finance have yielded substantial returns over the years.

Both Rakesh Jhunjhunwala and Radhakishan Damani have shown remarkable investing acumen, and their success stories inspire many aspiring investors in India. They exemplify the importance of careful research, a long-term investment approach, and the vision to spot promising opportunities.

Chapter 5: Doing Your Research

- How to analyze a company before investing.

Analyzing a company before investing is like exploring a magical world to see if it's worth buying tiny ownership potions (stocks) of that company. Here's a step-by-step procedure to help you become a skilled company explorer:

Step 1: Research the Company's Business
Start by understanding what the company does. Learn about its products, services, and the industry it operates in. Think about whether you believe in the company's mission and whether its business seems promising.

Step 2: Check the Company's Financials
Look at the company's financial statements, like the balance sheet, income statement, and cash flow statement. These are like treasure maps that show the company's financial health. Pay attention to things like revenue growth, profits, debts, and cash flow.

Step 3: Assess the Competitive Advantage
Find out if the company has a special magic that makes it stand out from its competitors. A strong competitive advantage, like a unique product or service, can make the company more likely to succeed.

Step 4: Study the Management Team
A good management team is like a group of skilled wizards leading the company. Research the key leaders and see if they have a strong track record and experience in running successful businesses.

Step 5: Analyze the Growth Prospects
Think about the company's potential for growth. Does it have plans
to expand its products, services, or markets? A company with
exciting growth prospects might be a good investment choice.

Step 6: Check for Risks
Every adventure has its risks, and so does investing. Identify the
potential risks that the company might face, like competition,
economic downturns, or changes in regulations. Consider how the
company plans to handle these risks.

Step 7: Look at Valuation
Valuation is like finding out if the tiny ownership potions (stocks) are
priced fairly. Compare the company's stock price to its earnings,
book value, and other industry metrics. A company that seems
undervalued might be a hidden gem.

Step 8: Read Analyst Reports and News
Seek guidance from other explorers (analysts) who study the
company. Read their reports and keep up with the latest news about
the company and its industry.

Step 9: Make Your Decision
Based on your research, decide if the company is worthy of your
investment. Remember that investing is like a journey, and you
might want to hold your tiny ownership potions (stocks) for a while.

Step 10: Diversify Your Adventures
Avoid putting all your magical coins into just one company. Diversify
your investments by buying tiny potions of different companies and
industries. It's like exploring many magical lands to spread your
risks.

Always remember, investing requires careful research and patience.
It's a skill that improves with practice.

- Important financial ratios to consider.

When investing in the stock market, financial ratios are like magical spells that help you understand a company's financial health and make more informed investment decisions. Here are some important financial ratios to consider:

1. Price-to-Earnings Ratio (P/E Ratio):
The P/E ratio compares a company's stock price to its earnings per share (EPS). It shows how much investors are willing to pay for each rupee of earnings. A lower P/E ratio may indicate that the stock is undervalued, while a higher P/E ratio could mean the stock is overvalued.

2. Price-to-Book Ratio (P/B Ratio):
The P/B ratio compares a company's stock price to its book value per share. Book value represents the net asset value of the company. A lower P/B ratio might suggest the stock is undervalued compared to its assets.

3. Dividend Yield:
Dividend yield is the annual dividend payment per share divided by the stock's current price. It shows the percentage return an investor gets from dividends alone. A higher dividend yield may be attractive for income-focused investors.

4. Debt-to-Equity Ratio:
The debt-to-equity ratio compares a company's total debt to its shareholders' equity. It reflects the company's financial leverage. A lower debt-to-equity ratio generally indicates a less risky investment.

5. Return on Equity (ROE):
ROE measures a company's profitability by showing how much profit it generates from shareholders' equity. A higher ROE is generally preferred, as it indicates efficient use of shareholders' investments.

6. Current Ratio:
The current ratio compares a company's current assets (e.g., cash, inventory) to its current liabilities (e.g., short-term debt). It assesses the company's ability to pay its short-term obligations. A current ratio above 1 indicates good short-term liquidity.

7. Debt-to-Asset Ratio:
The debt-to-asset ratio compares a company's total debt to its total assets. It shows the percentage of assets funded by debt. A lower debt-to-asset ratio is generally considered better, as it indicates lower financial risk.

8. Earnings Per Share (EPS):
EPS is a company's earnings divided by the number of outstanding shares. It shows how much profit a company is making per share. Increasing EPS over time may indicate growing profitability.

Remember, financial ratios provide valuable insights, but they are not the only factor to consider. It's essential to analyze a company's overall financial health, growth prospects, competitive advantage, and industry trends before making any investment decisions. As with any magical journey, conducting thorough research and seeking advice from experienced investors or financial advisors can enhance your investing success.

- Understanding company earnings and growth.

Understanding company earnings and growth is like following a magical story of a company's financial success. Let's explore what these terms mean and how they can help you make wise investment decisions:

1. Company Earnings:

Company earnings are like the treasure a company makes from its business activities. Just like counting the coins in your piggy bank, company earnings are the profits a company makes after deducting all its expenses from its total revenue.

- Revenue: Revenue is the total money the company makes from selling its products or providing its services. It's like the money you get from selling your toys or candies.

- Expenses: Expenses are the costs the company incurs to run its business, like salaries, raw materials, and other operating costs. Just like the money you spend on buying new toys or candies to sell.

- Profit: Profit is what's left after subtracting expenses from revenue. If the company earns more money than it spends, it makes a profit. Profit is like the extra money you have after selling all your toys or candies.

Analyzing a company's earnings helps you understand if the company is making money or facing financial challenges. Consistent and growing earnings over time are usually signs of a healthy and successful company.

2. Company Growth:
Company growth is like watching a tiny sapling grow into a giant tree over time. It shows how much the company is expanding its business and making progress.

- Revenue Growth: Revenue growth means the company is making more money over time. It's like the number of toys or candies you sell increasing year after year.

- Earnings Growth: Earnings growth shows how the company's profits are growing. Just like your piggy bank getting fuller and fuller as your savings increase.

- Expansion: Company growth may also involve expanding into new markets, launching new products, or acquiring other companies to become bigger and stronger.

When a company shows consistent and sustainable growth in its revenue and earnings, it indicates that the company is well-managed, and its products or services are in demand.

As an investor, understanding a company's earnings and growth is essential. A company with strong and growing earnings is like a magical potion that can increase the value of your tiny ownership potions (stocks) over time. But remember, like any good story, investing requires careful research and patience. Seek advice from experienced investors or financial advisors to help you uncover the most promising stories in the world of investments.

Chapter 6: Risks and Diversification

- What are the risks of investing?

Investing, like any magical adventure, comes with its fair share of risks. It's important to understand these risks before you embark on your investment journey. Here are some common risks of investing:

1. Market Risk: Market risk refers to the possibility that the overall stock market or specific asset classes might experience declines in value. Factors such as economic conditions, geopolitical events, or changes in investor sentiment can affect market prices.

2. Company-specific Risk: Company-specific risk is the risk associated with a particular company's performance. Factors like poor management, financial problems, or declining sales can affect the value of the company's stock.

3. Volatility Risk: Volatility risk is the risk of rapid and unpredictable price movements in the market. High volatility can lead to significant fluctuations in the value of investments.

4. Liquidity Risk: Liquidity risk is the risk of not being able to sell your investments quickly enough at a fair price. Some stocks or assets may have lower trading volumes, making it challenging to find buyers or sellers.

5. Currency Risk: Currency risk arises when investing in assets denominated in foreign currencies. Changes in exchange rates can impact the value of your investments.

6. Inflation Risk: Inflation risk refers to the possibility that the purchasing power of your money may decrease over time due to rising prices. Inflation can erode the value of your investments if they don't keep pace with the rate of inflation.

7. Interest Rate Risk: Interest rate risk occurs when changes in interest rates affect the value of fixed-income investments like bonds. When interest rates rise, bond prices typically fall, and vice versa.

8. Credit Risk: Credit risk is the risk of the borrower defaulting on their debt obligations. It applies to investments in bonds or other debt securities.

9. Regulatory Risk: Regulatory risk involves changes in government policies, laws, or regulations that can impact specific industries or companies.

10. Systematic Risk: Systematic risk, also known as non-diversifiable risk, is the risk that affects the entire market. It cannot be eliminated through diversification and is inherent to the investment environment.

Remember, every adventure has its challenges, and investing is no exception. However, with proper research, a long-term perspective, and a well-diversified portfolio, you can manage and mitigate some of these risks. It's essential to invest only the money you can afford to put at risk and seek advice from financial professionals to make informed decisions.

- The importance of diversification.

Diversification is like spreading your magical adventure across different lands, so you don't put all your treasures in one place. It's an essential strategy in investing that helps reduce risk and increase the chances of a successful journey. Here's why diversification is so important:

1. Risk Reduction: Just like you wouldn't want all your toys or candies in one basket, diversification helps spread your investments across various assets, such as different stocks, bonds, industries, or even countries. If one investment performs poorly, the others may balance it out, reducing the overall impact of losses.

2. Smoother Ride: By having a diversified portfolio, your investment journey becomes smoother. You're less likely to experience extreme ups and downs, like riding on a roller coaster, because the negative

impact of one investment is offset by the positive performance of others.

3. Exploiting Opportunities: Diversification allows you to take advantage of various opportunities in different markets. When one market or sector is doing well, your investments in that area can grow, even if other parts of your portfolio are not performing as strongly.

4. Protection Against Market Cycles: The economy and financial markets go through cycles of growth and downturns. Diversification helps you stay better protected during economic downturns, as your investments are not tied to a single market or industry.

5. Emotional Control: Having a diversified portfolio can help you feel more confident and in control of your investment journey. It reduces the urge to make impulsive decisions based on short-term market fluctuations.

6. Long-Term Growth: Diversification aligns with the idea of a long-term adventure. Over time, the potential for growth is enhanced by having a mix of different assets that can perform well under various economic conditions.

Remember, just like you carry different magical items and potions on your journey, diversification means having a well-balanced mix of investments. The actual level of diversification depends on your risk tolerance, investment goals, and time horizon.

Seek guidance from wise financial wizards or advisors to help you create a diversified portfolio that aligns with your unique adventure and goals.

- Building a diversified portfolio.

Building a diversified portfolio is like creating a magical shield that protects your investment journey from unexpected challenges. It's a crucial strategy for investors of all levels, and here's why it's so important:

1. Risk Reduction: The primary benefit of diversification is risk reduction. By investing in a variety of assets, such as stocks, bonds, real estate, and commodities, you spread your risk across different markets and industries. If one investment performs poorly, others may perform well, balancing out potential losses.

2. Smoother Performance: A diversified portfolio tends to experience less volatility and smoother performance over time. It helps avoid extreme highs and lows, making your investment journey less stressful.

3. Capturing Different Opportunities: Different assets perform well under various economic conditions. A diversified portfolio allows you to take advantage of different opportunities in both upturns and downturns.

4. Protection During Market Turbulence: Financial markets can be unpredictable. A diversified portfolio is like a shield that protects your investments during turbulent times, reducing the impact of negative events in any particular sector or asset class.

5. Long-Term Growth: Investing is a long-term journey. A well-diversified portfolio can provide steady growth over time, allowing your investments to compound and grow like a magical money tree.

6. Flexibility and Adaptability: Diversification provides flexibility to adjust your portfolio as your financial goals, risk tolerance, or economic conditions change. It allows you to adapt your strategy to meet your evolving needs.

7. Emotional Control: Diversification can help you stay focused on your long-term goals and prevent emotional decision-making during market fluctuations. It reduces the temptation to make impulsive moves based on short-term events.

8. Investment for the Future: Diversification is like planting seeds in different magical lands. It helps secure your financial future and provides a sense of security and stability for you and your family.

Remember, just like a skilled adventurer, building a diversified portfolio requires research, planning, and guidance from experienced financial wizards or advisors. Each portfolio will be unique to your individual goals, risk tolerance, and investment horizon.

By diversifying wisely, you can navigate the ups and downs of the financial world and increase the likelihood of achieving your investment goals.

Chapter 7: Stock Market Tips for Young Investors

- Avoiding common mistakes.

Avoiding common mistakes is like learning from the experiences of wise wizards who have faced challenges on their magical journeys. Here are some common investment mistakes and how to avoid them:

1. Lack of Research: Never rush into investments without understanding the company, industry, or asset class. Research thoroughly and seek guidance from experienced investors or financial advisors.

2. Emotional Investing: Avoid making investment decisions based on fear, greed, or short-term market fluctuations. Stay focused on your long-term goals and stick to your investment plan.

3. Putting All Eggs in One Basket: Diversify your investments to spread risk across various assets. Avoid putting all your money into a single stock or asset, as it can expose you to higher risks.

4. Chasing Quick Profits: Avoid falling for get-rich-quick schemes or investment fads. True investment success comes from patience, discipline, and a long-term approach.

5. Ignoring Risk Tolerance: Understand your risk tolerance and invest accordingly. Don't take on more risk than you can handle, as it may lead to panic selling during market downturns.

6. Market Timing: Trying to time the market (predicting when to buy or sell based on short-term market movements) is challenging and often counterproductive. Focus on long-term investing instead.

7. Overtrading: Excessive buying and selling of investments can lead to higher transaction costs and may not align with your long-term goals. Stick to a well-thought-out investment strategy.

8. Ignoring Fees and Expenses: Pay attention to the costs associated with investing. High fees can eat into your returns over time. Look for low-cost investment options.

9. Lack of Patience: Investing is a journey that requires time to grow. Avoid frequent checking of your investments and be patient, allowing your money to work its magic.

10. FOMO (Fear of Missing Out): Don't invest in something just because others are doing it. Make decisions based on your own research, risk tolerance, and financial goals.

11. Neglecting to Rebalance: Regularly review your portfolio and rebalance it if needed to maintain your desired asset allocation. This helps you stay on track with your investment strategy.

12. Not Having an Emergency Fund: Before investing, ensure you have an emergency fund to cover unexpected expenses. Avoid dipping into your investments during emergencies.

Remember, even the wisest wizards make mistakes, but learning from them can make you a better investor. Stay disciplined, be patient, and continue to educate yourself on the art of investing. Seek advice from financial advisors or experienced investors to navigate the magical world of investments successfully.

- Staying patient during market ups and downs.

Staying patient during market ups and downs is like holding onto the reins of your magical adventure, remaining calm, and trusting in the long-term journey. It's a crucial trait for successful investors, and here's why patience is so important:

1. Market Cycles Are Normal: Financial markets go through cycles of ups and downs. Just like the changing seasons, it's a natural part of the investment journey. Patience helps you weather the storm and wait for the sun to shine again.

2. Avoid Emotional Decisions: Patience prevents you from making impulsive decisions based on short-term market movements or fear of missing out. Emotions can lead to buying at the peak and selling at the bottom, hurting your overall returns.

3. Long-Term Perspective: Investing is a journey with long-term goals in mind. Being patient allows you to focus on the big picture and not get distracted by short-term noise.

4. Magic of Compounding: Patience allows the magic of compounding to work in your favor. By staying invested for the long term, your investments have more time to grow and multiply, like a powerful money spell.

5. Opportunity to Buy Low: During market downturns, prices of investments may drop. Patience gives you the chance to buy high-quality assets at lower prices, like finding a treasure on sale.

6. Riding Out Volatility: Market volatility is like riding on a bumpy magical road. Patience helps you stay steady during the ride and not panic when faced with short-term fluctuations.

7. Trust in Your Strategy: If you have done your research and crafted a well-thought-out investment strategy, patience allows you to trust in that strategy and stay the course.

8. Avoid Market Timing Mistakes: Trying to time the market is challenging and often leads to costly mistakes. Patience helps you avoid the temptation to make frequent changes based on market movements.

Remember, every magical adventure has its challenges, and the investment journey is no different. By staying patient, you can maintain a steady course and have the confidence to hold onto your investments during market ups and downs.

Seek guidance from experienced investors or financial advisors to stay focused and committed to your long-term goals. With patience and discipline, you'll be well-prepared to navigate the ever-changing financial landscape and unlock the true magic of investing.

- Tips for finding great investment opportunities.

Finding great investment opportunities is like seeking hidden treasures in the magical world of finance. Here are some tips to help you discover the most promising investments:

1. Conduct Thorough Research: Just like a skilled wizard, research is your magic wand. Study companies, industries, and asset classes you're interested in. Look for strong fundamentals, growth prospects, and competitive advantages.

2. Follow Market News: Stay updated with the latest financial news and market trends. Knowledge is a powerful spell that can help you spot potential opportunities before others do.

3. Analyze Financial Statements: Dive into the treasure chest of financial statements. Analyze company earnings, revenue growth, profit margins, and debt levels to assess the company's financial health.

4. Understand Industry Trends: Keep an eye on magical industry trends. Identify sectors with potential for growth and consider investing in companies that can benefit from those trends.

5. Seek Value: Look for undervalued assets that are selling for less than their true worth. Bargains can be like finding hidden gems that have the potential for significant returns.

6. Consider Dividends: Dividend-paying stocks can be like magical money potions that generate a steady income stream. Look for companies with a history of increasing dividends.

7. Focus on Quality: Quality investments are like enchanted items that can stand the test of time. Seek companies with strong management, good governance, and solid track records.

8. Diversify Wisely: Diversification is like spreading your magical powers across different lands. Build a well-diversified portfolio with a mix of assets to spread risk and capture opportunities.

9. Patience and Long-Term Vision: Like a patient wizard, be willing to hold onto your investments for the long term. Avoid getting swayed by short-term market fluctuations and focus on your long-term goals.

10. Seek Professional Advice: Just as you might consult with wise wizards, seek advice from experienced financial advisors. They can provide valuable insights and help you make informed decisions.

11. Assess Risk and Reward: Every adventure involves risk. Evaluate the potential risks and rewards of each investment opportunity and ensure they align with your risk tolerance.

12. Learn from Mistakes: Even the wisest wizards make mistakes. Learn from your investment experiences and continue to improve your skills as an investor.

Remember, investing is a journey that requires constant learning and adaptation. Be curious, stay disciplined, and seek wisdom from experienced investors to unlock the true magic of investing.

Chapter 8: Other Investment Options

- Introduction to bonds and mutual funds.

Bonds:

Bonds are like magical contracts where you lend money to a company, government, or organization in exchange for regular interest payments and the promise to get your money back at the end of the agreed-upon time. Bonds are considered a safer investment compared to stocks because they provide a fixed income and are generally less volatile.

Here's how bonds work:

1. Issuer: The entity that needs to borrow money, such as a government or a company, issues the bond.

2. Face Value: The face value or par value of the bond is the amount of money the issuer promises to pay back when the bond matures.

3. Coupon Rate: The coupon rate is the interest rate the issuer agrees to pay you annually on the face value of the bond.

4. Maturity: The maturity date is when the bond reaches its end, and the issuer repays the face value to the bondholder.

5. Buying and Selling: Bonds can be bought from the issuer during initial offerings or from other investors in the secondary market.

6. Credit Rating: Bonds are given credit ratings by rating agencies, indicating the issuer's ability to repay the debt. Higher-rated bonds are generally considered less risky.

Mutual Funds:

Mutual funds are like magical pools where many investors combine their money to be managed by a professional fund manager. The fund manager uses this money to invest in a diversified portfolio of stocks, bonds, or other assets. When you invest in a mutual fund, you own a share of the fund and participate in its gains and losses.

Here's how mutual funds work:

1. Diversification: Mutual funds offer instant diversification because your money is invested in a mix of different assets. This spreads risk and reduces the impact of a single investment's performance.

2. Professional Management: A skilled fund manager oversees the investments in the mutual fund, making decisions on which assets to buy or sell based on their expertise and research.

3. Types of Funds: Mutual funds come in different types, such as equity funds (investing in stocks), bond funds (investing in bonds), and balanced funds (a mix of stocks and bonds).

4. Net Asset Value (NAV): The price of a mutual fund share is based on its Net Asset Value, which is the total value of the fund's assets divided by the number of outstanding shares.

5. Liquidity: You can buy or sell mutual fund shares on any business day at the fund's NAV price. This provides easy access to your money when needed.

6. Fees and Expenses: Mutual funds charge fees, such as expense ratios, for managing the fund. It's essential to consider these costs when choosing a fund.

Both bonds and mutual funds offer unique benefits and can be valuable components of a diversified investment portfolio. As you embark on your investment journey, understanding these magical investment options will help you make informed decisions.

- Exploring index funds and ETFs.

Exploring index funds and ETFs is like discovering two magical tools that can help you invest in a wide range of assets with ease. Both index funds and ETFs offer diversification, cost-effectiveness, and simplicity. Let's dive into their magical properties:

Index Funds:

1. What Are They: Index funds are like enchanted baskets that aim to replicate the performance of a specific market index, such as the S&P 500. They hold a portfolio of assets (stocks or bonds) that matches the index's composition.

2. Diversification: Index funds offer instant diversification because they include a large number of assets within a single investment. This spreads risk and reduces the impact of any individual asset's performance.

3. Passive Management: Index funds are passively managed, meaning they don't rely on a fund manager's active decisions. Instead, they follow the index's composition and aim to match its performance.

4. Low Costs: Since index funds don't require active management, they typically have lower expenses compared to actively managed funds. This can translate to higher returns for investors.

5. Long-Term Investing: Index funds are well-suited for long-term investors who want to participate in the overall market growth without trying to beat it.

ETFs (Exchange-Traded Funds):

1. What Are They: ETFs are like magical hybrids between stocks and mutual funds. They are funds that trade on stock exchanges like individual stocks.

2. Diversification: Similar to index funds, ETFs provide diversification as they hold a basket of assets. They can track various indices, sectors, or asset classes.

3. Intraday Trading: ETFs can be bought and sold throughout the trading day at market prices, making them more flexible than mutual funds that are priced at the end of the day.

4. Cost-Effectiveness: ETFs also tend to have lower expenses due to their passive management structure, which can benefit investors.

5. Transparency: ETFs disclose their holdings daily, allowing investors to see exactly what assets are included in the fund.

6. Different Types: ETFs come in various types, including equity ETFs (tracking stock indices), bond ETFs (tracking bond indices), and commodity ETFs (tracking commodity prices).

Both index funds and ETFs are popular choices for beginner and seasoned investors alike, as they offer simplicity, diversification, and affordability. When choosing between the two, consider factors such as trading flexibility, fund expenses, and your investment goals.

Before embarking on your investment journey with these magical tools, it's always wise to conduct research and seek advice from experienced financial wizards or advisors.

- Saving for the future with a savings account.

Saving for the future with a savings account is like storing your magical treasures in a secure vault, ready to be used when needed. A savings account is a basic and essential financial tool that helps you set aside money for various goals and emergencies. Here's how it can be a powerful tool for your financial journey:

1. Safe and Secure: Like a strong magical shield, savings accounts are safe and insured by government agencies in many countries, protecting your money from loss.

2. Liquidity: Savings accounts provide easy access to your money whenever you need it. You can withdraw funds at any time without penalties, making it suitable for emergency expenses.

3. Earn Interest: Savings accounts earn interest on your deposited money, like a magical spell that makes your money grow over time. While the interest may be modest, it adds up over the long term.

4. No Market Risk: Unlike investments in the stock market or other assets, savings accounts are not subject to market fluctuations, providing stability for your funds.

5. Emergency Fund: A savings account is an excellent place to build an emergency fund. Having enough saved for unexpected expenses helps you avoid financial hardships during tough times.

6. Short-Term Goals: Savings accounts are perfect for saving money for short-term goals, like buying a new magical wand or going on a special adventure.

7. Easy to Set Up: Opening a savings account is a simple process that can be done at a local bank or online. Many banks offer low or no minimum balance requirements.

8. Teach Good Financial Habits: Saving regularly in a savings account helps you develop good financial habits and discipline in managing your money.

While savings accounts provide safety and liquidity, it's important to be aware of their limitations. The interest rates in savings accounts may be lower than inflation, which can erode your purchasing power over time. For long-term financial growth, consider combining a savings account with other investment options, such as stocks, bonds, or retirement accounts.

As you save for the future with a savings account, continue learning about different financial tools and strategies to make the most of your money's magical potential.

Chapter 9: Let's Get Started!

- Setting financial goals.

Setting financial goals is like mapping out your magical journey, with clear destinations and steps to reach them. It's an essential step in managing your finances and achieving your dreams. Here's how to set effective financial goals:

1. Identify Your Goals: Think about what you want to achieve with your money. Your goals could include saving for a magical adventure, buying a new wand, funding your education, starting a business, or preparing for the future.

2. Make Your Goals Specific: Define your goals clearly and precisely. For example, instead of saying "save money for a trip," specify the exact amount you need and the timeline you want to achieve it in.

3. Set Short-Term and Long-Term Goals: Create a mix of short-term goals (achievable within a year) and long-term goals (spanning several years). This allows you to celebrate achievements along the way while staying focused on the bigger picture.

4. Make Your Goals Realistic: While it's great to dream big, ensure your goals are attainable with your current financial situation. Setting unrealistic goals may lead to frustration and disappointment.

5. Assign Timeframes: Set deadlines for achieving each goal. Having a timeline creates a sense of urgency and helps you stay on track.

6. Prioritize Your Goals: Decide which goals are most important to you and rank them in order of priority. This will help you allocate your resources effectively.

7. Break Goals into Actionable Steps: Divide each goal into smaller, manageable tasks. Create a step-by-step plan to achieve them, like a magical recipe for success.

8. Review and Adjust: Regularly review your progress and adjust your goals if needed. Life is full of surprises, and it's okay to adapt your goals along the way.

9. Stay Committed: Like mastering magical spells, achieving financial goals requires dedication. Stay disciplined, and avoid temptations that may derail your progress.

10. Seek Support: Share your financial goals with friends, family, or a mentor. Having support and accountability can motivate you to stay focused on your journey.

Remember, setting financial goals is a powerful way to turn your dreams into reality. Be patient, and celebrate each milestone you achieve. By staying committed to your goals and practicing good financial habits, you'll unlock the true magic of financial success.

- Creating a budget to save for investments.

Creating a budget to save for investments is like creating a magical potion that helps you manage your money wisely and achieve your investment goals. Here's how to create an effective budget that allows you to save and invest for the future:

1. Assess Your Income: Start by calculating your total income. Include your salary, allowances, and any other sources of income you may have.

2. List Your Expenses: Make a list of all your expenses, including both fixed (e.g., rent, utilities, loan payments) and variable (e.g., groceries, entertainment) expenses. Track your spending for a few months to get an accurate picture.

3. Set Financial Goals: Determine how much money you want to save and invest. Define your short-term and long-term financial

goals, such as building an emergency fund or investing in the stock market.

4. Prioritize Your Goals: Rank your financial goals in order of priority. Decide how much money you want to allocate to each goal.

5. Create Categories: Divide your expenses into categories (e.g., housing, transportation, food) to better understand your spending patterns.

6. Allocate Funds: Allocate a portion of your income to each category, keeping in mind your financial goals. Be realistic and ensure you have enough funds for necessities and savings.

7. Cut Unnecessary Expenses: Identify areas where you can reduce spending. Eliminate non-essential expenses that don't align with your financial goals.

8. Pay Yourself First: Treat your savings and investments as a priority. Allocate a portion of your income to your investment fund before spending on other things.

9. Save Windfalls: Whenever you receive unexpected money, such as bonuses or gifts, consider saving a portion of it for investments.

10. Monitor and Adjust: Regularly review your budget and track your progress. Adjust your budget if necessary to ensure you're staying on track with your savings and investment goals.

11. Use Technology: Consider using budgeting apps or financial tools to help you track your expenses and manage your budget effectively.

12. Stay Disciplined: Like a skilled wizard, stick to your budget and avoid impulsive spending. Stay committed to your financial goals and the magic of compounding will work in your favor.

By creating a budget and sticking to it, you'll be able to save and invest for your future with confidence. Remember that every small contribution to your investment fund is like adding magic to your financial journey.

- Taking the first steps towards investing.

Taking the first steps towards investing is like embarking on a magical adventure into the world of finance. It can be exciting and a bit intimidating, but with careful planning and knowledge, you'll be well-prepared for your journey. Here are the essential steps to get started with investing:

1. Educate Yourself: Like a young wizard learning new spells, begin by educating yourself about different investment options, risk management, and the basics of the financial markets. Read books, articles, and take online courses to build your knowledge.

2. Set Clear Goals: Define your investment goals. Determine if you're investing for long-term wealth building, a specific purchase, retirement, or any other financial milestone.

3. Build an Emergency Fund: Before diving into investments, create an emergency fund to cover unexpected expenses. Aim for 3 to 6 months' worth of living expenses in a liquid and easily accessible account like a savings account.

4. Assess Your Risk Tolerance: Like knowing your magical strengths and limitations, understand your risk tolerance – your ability and willingness to handle fluctuations in investment values. Your risk tolerance will influence your investment choices.

5. Start Small: Begin with a modest amount that you're comfortable investing. As you gain experience and confidence, you can increase your investments over time.

6. Choose the Right Investment Account: Select the appropriate investment account, such as a brokerage account or retirement account like an IRA or 401(k), based on your goals and tax considerations.

7. Diversify Your Portfolio: Like a well-prepared adventurer, diversify your investments to spread risk. Consider a mix of stocks, bonds, and other asset classes to build a balanced portfolio.

8. Start with Index Funds or ETFs: Consider starting with low-cost index funds or exchange-traded funds (ETFs). These diversified investment options offer simplicity and broad exposure to the market.

9. Stay Committed to Your Plan: Like staying true to your magical quest, stay committed to your investment plan. Avoid making impulsive decisions based on short-term market fluctuations.

10. Review and Rebalance: Regularly review your investment portfolio and rebalance it if needed. This ensures that your investments align with your goals and risk tolerance.

11. Seek Professional Guidance: If you feel overwhelmed or uncertain, don't hesitate to seek advice from experienced financial advisors. They can help you navigate the complexities of investing and tailor a strategy to your needs.

Remember, investing is a journey that requires patience and discipline. The earlier you start, the more time your investments have to grow and work their magic.

Chapter 10: A Young Investor's Checklist

- Recap of the key points

Certainly! Here's a recap of the key points from our entire chat:

1. **Stock Market Investment **: The stock market is a place where people buy and sell shares of companies. Investing in the stock market means owning a small part of a company and hoping it grows in value over time.

2. **Importance of Investing**: Investing is important because it helps your money grow and gives you a chance to achieve your dreams and goals in the future.

3. **What is an Investment **: An investment is like planting a seed with your money, hoping it will grow into something bigger over time.

4. **Different Types of Investments **: Stocks are like owning a piece of a company, and bonds are like lending money to a company or government.

5. **Risk and Return in Investment **: Risk is like the chance of something not going as planned when you invest, and return is the money you earn or lose from your investment.

6. **What are Stocks **: Stocks are like owning a share or a part of a company. When you own a stock, you become a part-owner of that company.

7. **Famous Large Cap Companies in India and Past Performance**: Some famous large-cap companies in India include Reliance Industries, Tata Consultancy Services, and HDFC Bank, among others. Their past performance has been impressive, but it's essential to consider that past performance does not guarantee future results.

8. **Understanding Stock Prices and Ticker Symbols**: Stock prices represent the value of a company's shares, and ticker symbols are short codes used to identify each company's stock on the stock exchange.

9. **Choosing a Brokerage Account in India**: Select a brokerage account that offers user-friendly platforms, low fees, research tools, and good customer service.

10. **Placing Your First Stock Order**: Understand market orders (buying or selling at the current market price) and limit orders (setting a specific price to buy or sell).

11. **Understanding Market Orders and Limit Orders**: Market orders are like buying or selling immediately at the best available price, while limit orders are setting specific price levels to execute trades.

12. **Long-Term Investing**: Long-term investing means holding onto your investments for many years, giving them time to grow and reach their full potential.

13. **The Magic of Compounding**: Compounding is like a magical snowball effect where your money grows not only on the initial investment but also on the returns generated by that investment.

14. **Two Famous Investors and Success Stories in India**: Rakesh Jhunjhunwala and Radhakishan Damani are notable Indian investors with inspiring success stories.

15. **How to Analyze a Company Before Investing**: Analyzing a company involves researching its financial health, management, competitive position, and growth prospects.

16. **Important Financial Ratios**: Key financial ratios for investing include Price-to-Earnings (P/E) ratio, Debt-to-Equity (D/E) ratio, Return on Equity (ROE), and Current Ratio, among others.

17. **Understanding Company Earnings and Growth**: Company earnings refer to the money a company makes, and growth represents how fast the company is expanding.

18. **Risks of Investing**: Risks in investing include market risk, company-specific risk, volatility risk, inflation risk, and credit risk, among others.

19. **Importance of Diversification**: Diversification helps reduce risk by spreading investments across different assets and industries.

20. **Budgeting to Save for Investments**: Creating a budget ensures you have enough money to save and invest for your financial goals.

21. **Taking First Steps Towards Investing**: Educate yourself, set clear goals, build an emergency fund, assess your risk tolerance, and start small.

These key points are designed to help you begin your investment journey with confidence and knowledge. Remember to continue learning and seek guidance from experienced financial advisors to make informed decisions.

- A step-by-step checklist to follow.

Certainly! Here's a step-by-step checklist to follow as you embark on your magical investment journey:

Step 1: Set Financial Goals
- Define your short-term and long-term financial goals, such as buying a new wand, saving for a magical adventure, or planning for retirement.

Step 2: Assess Your Financial Situation
- Determine your current income, expenses, and savings. Understand your risk tolerance and time horizon for investments.

Step 3: Build an Emergency Fund
- Before investing, create an emergency fund with 3 to 6 months' worth of living expenses to cover unexpected costs.

Step 4: Educate Yourself

- Read books, articles, and take online courses to build your knowledge about investing and financial markets.

Step 5: Budget and Save
- Create a budget that allows you to save regularly for your investment goals. Pay yourself first by allocating a portion of your income to savings.

Step 6: Pay Off High-Interest Debt
- If you have high-interest debts, such as credit card debt, consider paying them off before investing. High-interest debts can erode potential investment returns.

Step 7: Establish an Investment Account
- Choose a suitable investment account, such as a brokerage account or retirement account, based on your goals and tax considerations.

Step 8: Start Small with Index Funds or ETFs
- Begin with low-cost index funds or exchange-traded funds (ETFs) to gain exposure to a diversified portfolio.

Step 9: Diversify Your Investments
- Allocate your investments across different asset classes (stocks, bonds, etc.) and industries to spread risk.

Step 10: Stay Committed to Your Plan
- Stick to your investment plan and avoid making impulsive decisions based on short-term market movements.

Step 11: Regularly Review and Rebalance
- Periodically review your investment portfolio and rebalance it if needed to maintain your desired asset allocation.

Step 12: Seek Professional Guidance (Optional)
- Consider seeking advice from experienced financial advisors for personalized investment strategies and guidance.

Step 13: Continue Learning and Adapting
- Keep educating yourself about investing and financial matters. Be open to adjusting your strategy as your financial situation and goals evolve.

Step 14: Be Patient and Stay Disciplined
- Investing is a long-term journey. Be patient and stay disciplined even during market ups and downs.

By following this step-by-step checklist, you'll be well-prepared to navigate the magical world of investing with confidence and wisdom. Remember, every small step counts, and with time, your investments will flourish like enchanted spells.

Start Your Stock Market Journey!

Starting early in investing is like harnessing the power of magic to unlock incredible financial potential. Let's explore the importance of starting early with a magical example:

Imagine two young wizards, Lily and James. Lily starts investing at the age of 25, while James decides to wait and begins investing at the age of 35. Both of them have a financial goal to save for their magical retirement, and they plan to invest $5,000 annually in the stock market.

Lily begins her investment journey at 25 and diligently invests $5,000 per year until she turns 35. After 10 years, she stops contributing any new money, but her investment continues to grow over time due to the magic of compounding.

James, on the other hand, waits until he turns 35 to start investing. He also invests $5,000 per year in the stock market, but he does so for a longer period of time, until he reaches 65.

Now, let's fast forward to their retirement at age 65. Both Lily and James have contributed a total of $50,000 each to their investments over the years. However, the magical power of starting early makes a significant difference in their investment outcomes.

Assuming an average annual return of 8% on their investments:

1. Lily (started at 25, invested for 10 years):
   - Total amount invested: $50,000
   - Value of her investment at 65: ~$863,812

2. James (started at 35, invested for 30 years):
   - Total amount invested: $150,000
   - Value of his investment at 65: ~$743,611

Despite investing three times the amount James did, Lily's investment has grown to be worth more due to the extra time her investments had to compound and grow.

This magical example illustrates the importance of starting early. The earlier you begin investing, the more time your money has to work its magic through compounding. Even with smaller contributions, starting early allows your investments to grow significantly over time.

By starting early, you have the potential to accumulate more wealth, achieve your financial goals faster, and secure a more comfortable and magical future. Don't underestimate the power of time in the world of investing. The sooner you take your first steps, the more magical your financial journey will become.

Dear young wizard of knowledge,

As you traverse the magical realm of learning, I urge you to embrace the enchantment of curiosity and the allure of constant growth. Like a never-ending journey through uncharted territories, the pursuit of knowledge is a wondrous adventure that knows no bounds.

The magical world is teeming with hidden treasures, awaiting discovery by those who dare to seek them. Every question you ask, every book you read, and every lesson you learn uncovers new spells and secrets that can shape your destiny. With each nugget of wisdom, you become a more powerful and enlightened wizard.

In your quest for knowledge, there are no limits to what you can achieve. Unleash your curiosity like a magical fire, burning brightly with a hunger to explore the unknown. Allow your mind to wander freely and dare to dream impossible dreams, for it is in the realm of curiosity that innovation and magic collide.

Remember, every great wizard throughout history started as a curious learner. They sought answers to questions no one else dared to ask, unlocking the deepest mysteries of the magical universe. Your thirst for knowledge can lead you down paths of unimaginable wonder and achievement.

In times of challenges and uncertainty, it is curiosity that lights the way forward. Embrace the joy of learning, for knowledge is like a guiding star, leading you through the darkest of nights.

Stay curious, young wizard, and never shy away from the pursuit of knowledge. The more you learn, the more your world expands, and the more you can make a difference in the lives of others and the magical realm around you.

So, let your imagination soar, ask the questions that stir your heart, and savor the knowledge you acquire. As you weave your own magical tale, let curiosity be your faithful companion, propelling you toward the realm of endless possibilities.

May your insatiable curiosity be the catalyst for a life filled with magic, wonder, and purpose.

With boundless encouragement and awe,

Your mentor of wisdom.

- A final note of inspiration for young investors.

Dear young investors,

As you embark on your magical journey into the realm of investing, I leave you with a final note of inspiration. You hold the power to shape your financial destiny and create a future brimming with enchanting possibilities.

Like skilled sorcerers, you have the ability to wield the magic of compounding. Embrace the power of starting early, for it ignites a spark that sets your investments on a course of extraordinary growth. With patience and discipline, watch your wealth multiply like a magical spell unfolding before your eyes.

Remember, every successful wizard faces challenges, but it is in facing those challenges that you gain the wisdom to overcome them. Embrace the lessons learned from both triumphs and setbacks, for they are the stepping stones on your path to prosperity.

Diversify your investments like gathering a treasure trove of magical artifacts. By spreading your wealth across different assets, you safeguard against the uncertainties of the financial world, ensuring your future remains secure and resilient.

Stay curious and thirst for knowledge, for it is through learning that you unlock the secrets of successful investing. Seek guidance from experienced mentors, explore the realms of financial wisdom, and cast spells of education that will guide you to informed decisions.

In times of turbulence and market fluctuations, remain steadfast in your convictions. Trust in your well-crafted investment plan, and resist the temptations of hasty decisions. Remember, the magic of long-term investing rewards those who stay true to their course.

Above all, cherish the journey of investing. Each step you take and each choice you make shapes your financial destiny. Embrace the thrill of seeing your wealth grow, not just for its material rewards, but for the sense of empowerment and accomplishment it brings.

As young investors, you possess the magic of time on your side. Utilize it wisely, and you will reap the rewards of your financial endeavors for years to come.

Now, go forth with courage and confidence. May your investments flourish, your dreams soar, and your financial future be filled with magic and abundance beyond measure.

With limitless inspiration and encouragement,

Your guide through the realm of investing.

Note: In this book, complex financial jargon has been avoided or explained in a way that is easy for a 10-year-old to understand. The aim is to provide basic and essential knowledge to spark curiosity and interest in the world of stock market investing. Always remember to seek guidance from a parent or guardian before making any financial decisions. Happy investing!

www.ingramcontent.com/pod-product-compliance
Lightning Source LLC
Chambersburg PA
CBHW071104260726
48661CB00006B/2450